Moto G Stylus 5G 2025 User Guide

A Complete Step-by-Step Manual for
Beginners and Seniors

Tova Greg

Table of Contents

Chapter 1...8

Getting Started with Your Moto G Stylus 5G...........................9

   Unboxing and First Impressions.....................................9

   What's in the Box..9

   Overview of Buttons and Ports.................................. 10

Chapter 2... 12

Setting Up Your Device...................................... 12

   Inserting SIM and SD Cards............................... 12

   What You'll Need:.. 12

   Steps to Insert SIM and SD Cards:.................. 12

   What Happens Next.................................... 13

   Initial Setup Walkthrough.............................. 14

   Creating or Signing into a Google Account...................... 17

   Why You Need a Google Account.............................. 17

   Managing Your Account Later...................................... 18

Chapter 3... 19

Navigating the Interface..................................... 19

   Understanding the Home Screen............................... 19

   Using the Notification Shade and Quick Settings........ 20

   Customizing the Home Screen and Widgets............... 21

   Managing Your Home Screen Layout.......................... 22

Chapter 4... 23

Understanding the Stylus.................................... 23

Stylus Features and Functions 23

Drawing and Taking Notes 24

Stylus Shortcuts and Apps 25

Stylus Settings and Customization 26

Chapter 5 27

Making and Receiving Calls.. 27

Dialing and Saving Contacts 27

Using Voicemail.. 28

Blocking Unwanted Numbers 29

Chapter 6 31

Sending Messages and Emails 31

Sending Text Messages.. 31

SMS and MMS Tips 31

Sending Text Messages.. 34

Using Google Messages App 34

Setting Up and Using Email.. 40

Setting Up Gmail on Your Moto G Stylus 5G 40

Setting Up Other Email Accounts (Outlook, Yahoo, etc.)
.... 41

Sending an Email.. 41

Organizing Your Emails 42

Searching for Emails.. 43

Managing Email Notifications 43

Adding and Removing Email Accounts 44

Chapter 7 46

Connecting to the Internet and Bluetooth 46

    Wi-Fi Setup and Management 46

    Using Mobile Data.. 47

    Pairing with Bluetooth Devices 48

    Troubleshooting Connectivity Issues 49

  Chapter 8: Using the Camera Like a Pro 51

    Camera Modes and Features...................................... 51

    Taking Photos and Videos 52

    Editing and Sharing Media 54

Chapter 9.. 56

Organizing Your Photos and Videos................................... 56

    Using Google Photos 56

    Creating Albums and Slideshows 58

    Backing Up Media to the Cloud 59

    Freeing Up Space on Your Device 60

  Chapter 10: Exploring Essential Apps............................. 61

    Calendar, Clock, and Calculator 61

    Files and Google Drive 63

    Using Play Store to Download Apps............................ 64

Chapter 11... 66

Using Google Assistant and Voice Commands.................... 66

    1. Activating Google Assistant..................................... 66

    2. Useful Commands for Everyday Tasks 67

    3. Voice Typing and Hands-Free Use............................ 69

Chapter 12 71

Battery Life and Power Management.............................71

    Checking Battery Usage 71

    Tips to Extend Battery Life....................................72

    Charging and Fast Charging Options.......................74

Chapter 13 76

Security and Privacy Settings.......................................76

    Fingerprint and Face Unlock..................................76

    Setting a Screen Lock 77

    Managing App Permissions....................................78

Chapter 14 81

Accessibility Features for Seniors 81

    Enlarging Text and Display Size..............................81

    High Contrast and Color Options............................82

    Using TalkBack and Magnification 83

Chapter 15 86

Storage and File Management.......................................86

    Checking Available Storage....................................86

    Moving Files to SD Card 87

    Cleaning Up Unused Apps and Files 88

Chapter 16 90

Troubleshooting Common Issues 90

    Phone Not Turning On 90

    Wi-Fi or Network Problems 91

App Crashes and Freezing 93

Chapter 17 95

Software Updates and Backups 95

Checking for System Updates 95

Backing Up Your Data 96

Factory Resetting the Phone 98

Chapter 18 99

Using the Moto App Features 99

Moto Gestures and Actions 99

Moto Display and Peek Display 100

Customizing with Moto Experiences 101

Chapter 19 104

Entertainment and Media 104

Listening to Music and Podcasts 104

Watching Videos and Streaming 106

Using FM Radio and YouTube 108

Chapter 20 109

Staying Safe Online 109

Recognizing Scams and Spam 109

Safe Browsing Tips 111

Using Parental Controls 112

Chapter 21 115

Helpful Tips and Tricks 115

Screenshot and Screen Recording 115

Split Screen and Multitasking 116

Hidden Features You Should Know.............117

Chapter 22 120

Appendix and FAQs.....................................120

Glossary of Common Terms.......................120

Frequently Asked Questions (FAQs) 121

Customer Support and Resources 123

Chapter 1

Getting Started with Your Moto G Stylus 5G

Unboxing and First Impressions

Opening a brand-new device is always exciting, and the Moto G Stylus 5G (2025) does not disappoint. As you lift the lid, you're greeted by a sleek, modern smartphone that feels solid and premium in your hand. The large display, slim bezels, and built-in stylus all give the phone a high-end look and feel.

Before powering it on, take a moment to appreciate the craftsmanship and design. The back has a smooth finish, and the camera module is neatly arranged. You'll notice the stylus is discreetly housed in the bottom-right corner—easy to access, yet secure.

What's in the Box

Here's what you can typically expect inside the box:

- **Moto G Stylus 5G (2025) smartphone**

- **Built-in stylus** (already inserted in the phone)
- **USB-C charging cable**
- **Wall adapter for charging**
- **SIM ejector tool**
- **Quick Start Guide and Safety Information**
- **Protective case** (included in some regions)
- **Screen protector (pre-applied)**

Tip: Keep the box and accessories together—you may need them later for troubleshooting or warranty service.

Overview of Buttons and Ports

Familiarizing yourself with the physical layout of your phone makes everyday use smoother. Here's a quick guide:

- **Power Button**
  Located on the right side. Press once to wake or lock the screen. Hold to power off or restart.
- **Volume Buttons**
  Just above the power button. Use to adjust volume during calls, media playback, or system sounds.
- **Stylus Slot**
  Bottom-right corner. Gently press in to release the stylus.
- **USB-C Charging Port**
  Centered at the bottom. Used for charging and data transfer.
- **Headphone Jack**
  Still available! Found on the bottom-left corner—plug in standard 3.5mm headphones.
- **Microphone and Speaker**
  Located at the top and bottom for calls and audio output.

- **SIM Card Tray**
  On the left side of the phone. Use the SIM ejector tool to access.
- **Rear Camera Module**
  Found on the back. Includes the main camera, ultrawide lens, and flash.

Chapter 2

Setting Up Your Device

Inserting SIM and SD Cards

Before you can make calls, send texts, or use mobile data, you'll need to insert your SIM card. If you plan to expand your storage, this is also the time to insert a microSD card.

What You'll Need:

- Moto G Stylus 5G (2025) smartphone
- SIM ejector tool (included in the box) or a small paperclip
- Nano SIM card from your carrier
- Optional: microSD card (for extra storage)

Steps to Insert SIM and SD Cards:

1. **Power Off Your Phone**
   It's best to turn off your phone before inserting or removing any cards to avoid damage or errors.
2. **Locate the SIM Tray**
   The SIM tray is on the **left side** of the phone. Look for a small pinhole next to a thin tray outline.
3. **Eject the Tray**
   Insert the SIM ejector tool (or unfolded paperclip) into the pinhole and apply a little pressure. The tray will pop out slightly—gently pull it out the rest of the way.

4. **Place the SIM Card**

- The tray has a dedicated slot for the **Nano SIM card**.
- Match the angled corner of the SIM card with the tray's shape.
- The gold contacts should face **down**.

5. **Insert the microSD Card (Optional)**

- If you're using a microSD card for extra storage, place it in the second slot.
- Again, make sure the gold contacts are facing **down**.

6. **Reinsert the Tray**
   Carefully slide the tray back into the phone. It should go in smoothly—do not force it.
7. **Turn the Phone Back On**
   Press and hold the power button until the Moto logo appears. Your phone will begin reading the SIM and SD cards.

What Happens Next

- If your SIM is active, your phone will automatically connect to your mobile network.
- If you inserted a microSD card, the phone may prompt you to set it up as portable or internal storage.

Tip: If your phone doesn't recognize the SIM card, restart the device or check that it's placed correctly in the tray.

Once your SIM and SD cards are inserted and your Moto G Stylus 5G (2025) is powered on, it's time to go through the initial setup. This process helps you get your phone ready for use and customize it to your needs.

Follow these steps to set up your device with ease:

1. Choose Your Language

- The first screen lets you choose your **preferred language**.
- Tap the arrow to proceed once your language is selected.

2. Connect to Wi-Fi

- If you're in range of a Wi-Fi network, select it and enter the password.
- Connecting to Wi-Fi now helps the phone check for updates and set up your account faster.
- You can skip this step if you prefer to use mobile data.

Tip: Using Wi-Fi saves mobile data during setup, especially when restoring apps or downloading updates.

3. Insert SIM (if not already done)

- If you skipped the SIM card earlier, you'll be prompted to insert it.

14

- You can also skip and insert it later—Wi-Fi will still allow you to proceed.

4. Copy Apps and Data (Optional)

- You can **copy apps, photos, and settings** from your old phone.
- Choose:

1. **"Copy apps & data"** if you have an older phone nearby.
2. Or select **"Don't copy"** if you want a fresh start.

5. Sign in to Google Account

- Signing in to your **Google account** allows you to access Gmail, YouTube, Google Photos, the Play Store, and more.
- You can skip this step if you don't have an account yet—you can always sign in later.

Tip: Use a secure password or passphrase for your Google account to keep your data safe.

6. Set Up a Screen Lock

- Choose how you want to **secure your phone**:

a) Pattern
b) PIN
c) Password
d) Or set up **Fingerprint or Face Unlock** (can also be done later).

7. Enable or Skip Google Services

You'll be asked to review several options, including:

- Backing up data to Google Drive
- Location access
- Allowing Google to scan for security threats
- Using voice services like "Hey Google"

You can toggle each option ON or OFF, then tap **"Accept"** to continue.

8. Set Up Stylus Features (Optional)

- Moto will give you an intro to the stylus and show how it works.
- You can enable shortcuts like **Notes, Screenshot, and Magnify** with the stylus right from the start.

9. Add Finishing Touches

- You may be asked to choose your system theme (light or dark mode).
- You can also adjust font size, enable accessibility features, or personalize your wallpaper.

10. Welcome to Your Moto G Stylus 5G!

- Once setup is complete, you'll land on the **Home Screen**.
- From here, you're ready to explore, install apps, and make the phone truly yours.

A Google account is essential for getting the most out of your Moto G Stylus 5G (2025). It gives you access to important apps and services like Gmail, Google Photos, Google Maps, YouTube, the Play Store, and backup features.

You can either sign in with an existing account or create a new one directly from your phone during setup.

Why You Need a Google Account

With a Google account, you can:

- **Download apps** from the Google Play Store
- **Sync your contacts, photos, and calendar**
- **Back up your data automatically**
- Use **Google Assistant, Drive, Docs, YouTube, and more**

Option 1: Sign In to an Existing Account

1. When prompted during setup, tap **"Sign in"**.
2. Enter your **email address** (e.g., yourname@gmail.com) and tap **Next**.
3. Type your **password** and tap **Next** again.
4. Review Google's terms and privacy info, then tap **"I agree"**.

That's it! Your account will now sync automatically, and you can access your Gmail, Drive, Photos, and more.

Option 2: Create a New Google Account

If you don't have a Google account yet:

1. Tap **"Create account"** when prompted.
2. Choose **"For myself"** or **"For my child"**.
3. Enter your **first and last name**, then tap **Next**.
4. Add your **birthdate and gender**, then tap **Next**.
5. Choose a **Gmail address** from suggestions or create your own.
6. Set a secure **password** (use a mix of letters, numbers, and symbols).
7. Add a **phone number** (optional, but useful for recovery).
8. Accept the terms and conditions.

Managing Your Account Later

If you skip signing in during setup, you can add a Google account later by:

- Going to **Settings**
- Tapping **Accounts > Add account > Google**
- Following the same sign-in or sign-up steps

Tip: Write down your Gmail and password and store it in a safe place. You'll need it if you ever reset your phone or switch devices.

Chapter 3

Navigating the Interface

Once your Moto G Stylus 5G (2025) is set up, it's time to get familiar with the interface. The user interface on your phone is designed to be intuitive, but knowing how to navigate it efficiently will make your experience smoother and more enjoyable.

Understanding the Home Screen

The Home Screen is where most of your daily interactions with the phone happen. It's where you access apps, widgets, and features quickly. Here's what you'll find:

1. **App Icons**: All of your apps are represented by icons. These can be arranged in any order you like. Simply tap an app to open it.
2. **Search Bar**: At the top of the screen, you'll see a **Google Search bar**. Use it to search the web, your apps, or even your phone.
3. **Dock**: The **Dock** at the bottom holds your most-used apps for easy access. These apps stay visible on every Home Screen page.
4. **Pages**: The Home Screen is made up of several pages. To switch between pages, swipe left or right. You can add more pages, remove pages, and even set a wallpaper for each.

5. **App Drawer**: To access all installed apps, swipe **up** from the bottom of the screen. This is where you'll find every app on your phone.

Using the Notification Shade and Quick Settings

The Notification Shade and Quick Settings are essential for quickly managing your phone's functions.

Notification Shade

To view your notifications (like messages, app alerts, and calls):

1. **Swipe down** from the top of the screen.
2. Your notifications will appear, and you can scroll down to see them all.
3. Tap any notification to open it. To clear a notification, swipe it away to the side.

Tip: You can expand or collapse certain notifications (e.g., messages, emails) by swiping down further or tapping on them.

Quick Settings

Quick Settings gives you instant control over common features like Wi-Fi, Bluetooth, and brightness. To access it:

1. **Swipe down** again (after the Notification Shade) to reveal the Quick Settings menu.

2. Here you'll find shortcuts for Wi-Fi, Bluetooth, Do Not Disturb, Airplane Mode, Battery Saver, and more.
3. You can **tap** any icon to enable/disable that feature.
4. To access more options, tap the **gear icon** to open **Settings**.

*Tip: You can customize the Quick Settings tiles to prioritize the tools you use most often. Just tap the **pencil icon** when in the Quick Settings menu.*

Customizing the Home Screen and Widgets

Your Home Screen is yours to personalize. Here are some ways to make it fit your style and needs.

Changing the Wallpaper

1. Tap and **hold** on an empty space on the Home Screen.
2. Select **Wallpapers**.
3. Choose from your gallery or the default options, including animated wallpapers or static images.

Adding Apps and Folders

1. **To add apps**: Open the **App Drawer**, tap and **hold** an app icon, then drag it to your desired position on the Home Screen.
2. **To create a folder**: Tap and **hold** an app, then drag it on top of another app. A folder will be created. You can rename the folder by tapping on its name.

21

Widgets are small apps or features that live directly on your Home Screen, giving you quick access to info or controls without opening the full app.

1. **To add a widget**: Tap and **hold** an empty space on the Home Screen.
2. Select **Widgets** from the options.
3. Browse the available widgets and tap the one you want to add.
4. Drag it to your desired location on the Home Screen.

Pro Tip: Some widgets can be resized by tapping and holding the widget and dragging the edges to adjust its size.

Managing Your Home Screen Layout

If you want to tidy up your layout or make it more functional:

- **Remove apps or widgets** by tapping and holding them, then selecting **Remove**.
- **Rearrange apps** by tapping and holding any app icon, then dragging it to a new position.
- **Adjust icon size** and grid settings: Go to **Settings > Display > Advanced > Icon Size**.

Chapter 4

Understanding the Stylus

The built-in stylus on your Moto G Stylus 5G (2025) isn't just a cool accessory; it's a powerful tool that can enhance your productivity, creativity, and overall user experience. Whether you're jotting down quick notes, drawing sketches, or navigating your phone, the stylus provides precision and convenience.

Stylus Features and Functions

The Moto G Stylus 5G's stylus is equipped with several handy features to make your device more interactive and intuitive.

1. **Precision Input**: The stylus offers a fine tip, providing accuracy for writing, drawing, and tapping small icons.
2. **No Need for Charging**: Unlike some other stylus devices, the Moto G Stylus 5G doesn't require charging, meaning you never have to worry about it running out of battery.
3. **Pressure Sensitivity**: The stylus is sensitive to varying pressure levels, allowing for natural writing and drawing. The harder you press, the thicker the line you draw.
4. **Built-In Storage**: The stylus is securely stored in a slot on the bottom-right of the phone. It's easily accessible but stays tucked away when not in use.

5. **Stylus Detection**: As soon as the stylus is removed from the slot, the phone recognizes it and will often prompt you with stylus-related tools.

Drawing and Taking Notes

The Moto G Stylus 5G is perfect for creative tasks like drawing or taking handwritten notes, making it a versatile tool for both work and play.

1. Taking Notes with the Stylus

You can quickly start writing notes without opening an app:

1. **Remove the Stylus** from the slot.
2. **Tap on the screen** to open the **Moto Note** feature.
3. Start **writing directly on the screen**! No need to unlock your phone or open an app.
4. You can switch between different note-taking tools, including pen, highlighter, and eraser, by tapping on the options at the top of the screen.
5. **Save your note** by tapping the **save icon** once you're done.

Pro Tip: You can draw and write on screenshots too! Just open a photo, press the stylus icon, and start annotating.

2. Drawing with the Stylus

For a more artistic experience, use your stylus with drawing apps like **Adobe Illustrator Draw** or **Autodesk SketchBook**:

1. **Open your drawing app**.

2. Select the tool (brush, pencil, etc.) that you want to use and adjust the thickness of the lines.
3. Use your stylus to draw with precision. You can even apply different pressure levels for shading and detailing.

Tip: Try out apps that support pressure sensitivity for a more realistic drawing experience.

Stylus Shortcuts and Apps

The Moto G Stylus 5G comes with several built-in shortcuts and features that make using the stylus even easier.

1. Moto Actions and Gestures

- **Quick Screenshot**:
  When you remove the stylus from its slot, the **Quick Capture** feature can automatically take a screenshot and let you annotate it right away.
- **Screen Off Memo**:
  This is one of the most useful features for quick note-taking. If your phone's screen is off, just **remove the stylus** and start writing directly on the screen. The phone will automatically save the note.
- **Glance Feature**:
  Use the stylus to interact with your phone even when it's locked. With **Moto Display**, you can tap the screen with the stylus to check the time, notifications, or calendar without unlocking the phone.

There are several apps available that can take full advantage of the stylus:

- **Moto Note**: For quick note-taking and memo writing.
- **Google Keep**: A simple, easy-to-use note-taking app that lets you draw and write notes.
- **OneNote**: For detailed note-taking, syncing across devices, and organizing notes.
- **Adobe Photoshop Sketch**: For more advanced drawing with layers and rich brush options.
- **Autodesk SketchBook**: A professional drawing app that supports pressure sensitivity.

Pro Tip: You can set your favorite stylus apps to open automatically when the stylus is removed from its slot by going to Settings > Moto > Moto Actions.

Stylus Settings and Customization

You can further customize your stylus features:

1. Go to **Settings** > **Moto** > **Moto Actions**.
2. Here, you can adjust shortcuts like **Quick Capture**, **Screen Off Memo**, and **One-Touch Start for Notes**.

Chapter 5

Making and Receiving Calls

Your Moto G Stylus 5G (2025) makes it easy to stay connected with friends, family, and colleagues. This chapter walks you through the basics of making and receiving calls, saving contacts, using voicemail, and blocking unwanted numbers.

Dialing and Saving Contacts

Making a call and managing contacts is straightforward on your Moto G Stylus 5G.

1. Making a Call

- **Dialing Directly:**
    1. Open the **Phone app** by tapping the green phone icon.
    2. Tap the **dialpad icon** (the numbers) in the bottom-right corner.
    3. Enter the phone number and press the green **call button**.
- **Calling a Saved Contact:**
    1. Open the **Phone app**.
    2. Tap **Contacts** at the bottom of the screen.
    3. Scroll or use the search bar to find the contact you want to call.

4. Tap the contact's name, then tap the phone number you wish to call.

*Pro Tip: You can also **use voice dialing** by tapping the microphone icon in the dialer and saying the contact's name.*

2. Saving a Contact

To save a contact for easy future calling:

1. Open the **Phone app**.
2. Tap **Contacts** > **Create new contact**.
3. Enter the contact's **name** and **phone number**.
4. Optionally, you can add additional details, like an email address, photo, and address.
5. Tap **Save** when done.

Tip: If the contact is already in your Google account, it will automatically sync across all your devices.

Using Voicemail

Voicemail is an essential feature for when you're unable to answer a call.

1. Setting Up Voicemail

To set up voicemail:

1. Open the **Phone app**.
2. Tap the **three-dot menu** in the top-right corner.
3. Tap **Settings** > **Voicemail**.
4. Follow the prompts to set up your voicemail greeting and PIN (if required).

Tip: If your carrier supports visual voicemail, you can view and listen to messages directly in the Phone app, making it more convenient than dialing into your voicemail inbox.

2. Checking Voicemail

To check your voicemail:

1. Open the **Phone app**.
2. Tap the **Voicemail** tab at the bottom.
3. Tap on any message to listen to it. You can save or delete messages as needed.

Pro Tip: You can change your voicemail greeting by following the prompts when checking voicemail or going into voicemail settings.

Blocking Unwanted Numbers

No one likes spam or unwanted calls. Fortunately, your Moto G Stylus 5G has built-in features for blocking numbers.

1. Blocking a Call Directly

To block a number from your call history:

1. Open the **Phone app** and go to your **Recents** or **Contacts**.
2. Find the phone number you want to block.
3. Tap on the number or contact, then tap the **three-dot menu** in the top-right corner.
4. Select **Block number** and confirm.

2. Blocking Numbers via Settings

To block numbers manually:

1. Open the **Phone app**.
2. Tap the **three-dot menu** in the top-right corner and choose **Settings**.
3. Tap **Blocked numbers**.
4. Tap **Add a number** and enter the phone number you wish to block.

Tip: If you're receiving a lot of spam calls, you can also enable **Caller ID and Spam protection** *from the Phone settings to help filter out potential spam calls.*

3. Unblocking a Number

To unblock a number:

1. Open the **Phone app** and go to **Settings** > **Blocked numbers**.
2. Tap the **X** next to the number you want to unblock.

Chapter 6

Sending Messages and Emails

Sending Text Messages

Texting is one of the most common ways to stay connected. With your Moto G Stylus 5G, sending and receiving SMS (Short Message Service) and MMS (Multimedia Messaging Service) messages is quick and easy. This section provides helpful tips for both SMS and MMS messaging.

SMS and MMS Tips

1. Sending a Simple Text (SMS)

To send a text message using SMS:

1. Open the **Messages app**.
2. Tap the **+ icon** or **Start chat** at the bottom-right of the screen.
3. Enter the recipient's phone number or tap the **Contacts icon** to select a saved contact.
4. Type your message in the text field at the bottom.
5. Tap the **send icon** (the paper plane) to send your message.

*Tip: If you're sending a message to a group, tap **+ Add people** in the recipient field to add multiple contacts.*

2. Sending Multimedia Messages (MMS)

MMS allows you to send images, videos, and audio clips along with your text message. Here's how to send one:

1. Open the **Messages app**.
2. Tap the **+ icon** or **Start chat**.
3. Enter the recipient's phone number or select a contact.
4. Tap the **paperclip icon** next to the text field.
5. Choose whether you want to attach a **photo**, **video**, or **audio file**.
6. Select the media you want to send and tap **Done**.
7. Type your message (if desired) and tap the **send icon**.

*Pro Tip: To send a photo or video directly from your camera, tap the **camera icon** instead of the paperclip to take a picture or record a video and send it instantly.*

3. Group Messaging

Sending a group message is a great way to stay connected with multiple people at once. Here's how to do it:

1. Open the **Messages app**.
2. Tap the **+ icon** or **Start chat**.
3. In the recipient field, type the names of multiple contacts or tap the **Contacts icon** to add people.
4. Type your message in the text field.
5. Tap the **send icon**.

*Tip: If you're sending a large group message with photos or videos, ensure you have **MMS** enabled, as SMS will not support multimedia files.*

4. Enabling/Disabling MMS Auto-Download

By default, MMS media (images, videos) will automatically download when you receive a message. If you'd prefer to download MMS manually to save data, follow these steps:

1. Open the **Messages app**.
2. Tap the **three-dot menu** in the top-right corner.
3. Tap **Settings > Advanced**.
4. Toggle **Auto-download MMS** to **Off** to manually download MMS content.

Tip: Turning off auto-download is great for saving mobile data, especially if you're on a limited plan.

5. Using Rich Communication Services (RCS)

RCS is a newer messaging protocol that allows for features like read receipts, typing indicators, and sending high-quality media. To use RCS on your Moto G Stylus 5G:

1. Open the **Messages app**.
2. Tap the **three-dot menu > Settings**.
3. Tap **Chat features** and enable **Enable chat features**.
4. Your phone will automatically switch to RCS, and you can start enjoying enhanced messaging features.

Tip: RCS requires an internet connection and is available between compatible devices. It's similar to popular messaging apps like WhatsApp or iMessage but integrated into your default SMS/MMS app.

To add fun to your messages, use emojis, stickers, or GIFs:

- **Emojis**: Tap the **smiley face icon** on the keyboard to bring up the emoji panel.
- **GIFs**: Tap the **GIF icon** to search for and add GIFs to your message.
- **Stickers**: Some apps (like Google Messages) have sticker packs you can download for even more personalization.

Pro Tip: You can add frequently-used emojis or create custom emoji shortcuts in the keyboard settings to make texting faster.

If you want to remove or organize your messages:

- **Delete a message**: Tap and **hold** the message, then tap **Delete**.
- **Delete a conversation**: Tap and **hold** the conversation thread, then select **Delete**.
- **Archive a conversation**: Swipe the conversation to the left or right to archive it, keeping it out of your main inbox but accessible when needed.

Sending Text Messages

Using Google Messages App

The **Google Messages app** is the default messaging app on your Moto G Stylus 5G, and it's packed with features that make texting and multimedia sharing easier, faster, and more enjoyable. This section will guide you through the essential features of the Google Messages app.

1. Setting Up Google Messages as Your Default Messaging App

If the Google Messages app is not already set as your default messaging app, follow these steps:

1. Open the **Settings app**.
2. Tap **Apps > Default apps**.
3. Under **SMS app**, select **Messages** to make it your default messaging app.

Tip: Google Messages offers a clean, easy-to-use interface, and it's compatible with features like RCS (Rich Communication Services) for enhanced messaging.

2. Composing and Sending Messages

Once you've set up the app, here's how to send a message:

1. Open the **Messages app**.
2. Tap the **+** or **Start chat** at the bottom-right corner.
3. Enter the contact's name or phone number.
4. Type your message in the text field.
5. If you want to attach a photo, video, or audio, tap the **paperclip icon** (next to the text field) to attach multimedia.

6. Tap the **send icon** (the paper plane) to send your message.

Tip: Google Messages allows you to send high-quality images and videos, especially if you use RCS for better multimedia support.

3. Using Rich Communication Services (RCS)

RCS enhances your messaging experience with features like read receipts, typing indicators, high-quality media sharing, and more. To enable RCS in Google Messages:

1. Open the **Messages app**.
2. Tap the **three dots** in the top-right corner and select **Settings**.
3. Tap **Chat features**.
4. Toggle on **Enable chat features** to activate RCS.

Once activated, you'll see enhanced messaging features when texting other RCS-enabled users.

Note: RCS requires an internet connection (Wi-Fi or mobile data) and works between users with RCS-enabled phones and services.

4. Organizing and Managing Conversations

The Google Messages app makes it easy to organize and manage your conversations:

Pinning Conversations

1. Open the **Messages app**.
2. Tap and **hold** on a conversation.
3. Tap **Pin** to keep important conversations at the top of your list for easy access.

Archiving Conversations

1. To keep your inbox tidy, swipe left or right on a conversation to **archive it**.
2. Archived messages won't show up in your main inbox but are still accessible in the **Archived** section.

Deleting Conversations

1. Tap and **hold** the conversation you want to delete.
2. Tap **Delete** to remove it from your inbox.

Tip: Archiving keeps conversations organized without losing them, while deleting permanently removes them.

5. Sending GIFs, Emojis, and Stickers

Adding some fun to your conversations is easy with Google Messages. Here's how to do it:

- **Emojis:** Tap the **smiley face icon** on the keyboard to bring up emojis. Select the emoji you want to use, and it will be inserted into the text field.
- **GIFs:** Tap the **GIF icon** (a square icon with a small play button) to search for and send GIFs.
- **Stickers:** Tap the **sticker icon** (a smiling face or a sticker icon) to send personalized stickers.

*Pro Tip: You can also download additional sticker packs through the **Google Play Store** for even more variety.*

6. Sending and Receiving Multimedia Messages (MMS)

Google Messages supports MMS for sending pictures, videos, and audio files. To send multimedia messages:

1. Tap the **paperclip icon** next to the text field.
2. Select **Gallery** to choose a photo or video from your collection, or select **Camera** to take a new photo or video.
3. Once your media is attached, tap **Send**.

Tip: MMS allows you to send photos and videos up to 100MB, but be mindful of your data usage if you're not connected to Wi-Fi.

7. Using Google Messages for Web

You can also send and receive text messages from your computer using **Google Messages for Web**:

1. Open **Google Messages** on your phone.
2. Tap the **three dots** > **Messages for web**.
3. Scan the QR code on **messages.google.com/web** using your phone.
4. You can now send and receive texts from your computer, with all the same features as the app.

Pro Tip: Google Messages for Web is perfect for typing long messages on a keyboard while still having the convenience of using your phone's text history.

8. Enabling or Disabling Notifications

You can adjust notifications to make sure you don't miss important messages or to reduce distractions:

1. Open the **Messages app**.
2. Tap the **three dots** > **Settings**.
3. Tap **Notifications** and toggle them on or off as needed.
4. You can customize the type of notifications, including sound, vibration, and pop-ups.

Tip: You can also mute conversations for specific chats so they won't send notifications while keeping other chats active.

9. Searching for Messages

If you're looking for a specific message, use the search function in Google Messages:

1. Open the **Messages app**.
2. Tap the **search bar** at the top of the screen.
3. Enter keywords, contact names, or phone numbers to find the message you're looking for.

Tip: Search makes it easy to locate old conversations or specific content, such as photos or links.

Staying connected through email is a vital part of your daily communication. On your Moto G Stylus 5G, setting up and using email is easy, whether you're using Gmail, Outlook, or any other email service. This chapter will walk you through the steps to set up your email accounts and manage them efficiently.

Setting Up Gmail on Your Moto G Stylus 5G

Since Gmail is the default email app for most Android devices, setting it up on your Moto G Stylus 5G is simple. Here's how:

1. **Open the Gmail app**: It's pre-installed on your device. You can find it in your apps drawer or on your home screen.
2. **Sign In**:

- If you're signing in for the first time, tap **Sign in**.
- Enter your Google email address (e.g., example@gmail.com) and tap **Next**.
- Enter your password and tap **Next** to complete the sign-in process.

3. **Sync Your Account**: Once signed in, Gmail will automatically sync with your account, pulling in all your emails and contacts.

Pro Tip: If you have multiple Gmail accounts, you can easily switch between them by tapping your profile picture in the top-right corner of the app.

Setting Up Other Email Accounts (Outlook, Yahoo, etc.)

To set up email accounts from other providers like Yahoo, Outlook, or any IMAP/POP account, follow these steps:

1. **Open the Gmail app** (or **Email app** if you prefer).
2. Tap the **three-line menu** icon in the top-left corner.
3. Scroll down and tap **Settings**.
4. Tap **Add account**.
5. Choose your email provider from the list, or select **Other** to manually enter server settings.
6. Enter your **email address** and **password**, and follow the on-screen prompts to complete the setup. If you're using a provider like Outlook or Yahoo, Gmail will usually configure the settings automatically.
7. Once done, your emails will start syncing, and you can start managing them.

Tip: If you're setting up an IMAP or POP account manually, make sure to have your provider's incoming and outgoing server settings handy (such as mail server address, port number, etc.).

Sending an Email

To send an email from your Gmail or any other email app:

1. Open the **Gmail** or **Email app**.
2. Tap the **Compose icon** (usually a **pencil** or + sign) at the bottom-right of the screen.
3. In the **To** field, enter the recipient's email address.
4. In the **Subject** field, enter the subject of your email.
5. Tap the **body** of the email to type your message.

6. When you're ready to send, tap the **Send** button (usually an **arrow** or **paper plane**).

*Pro Tip: You can attach files like documents, images, and videos by tapping the **paperclip icon** and selecting your files.*

Organizing Your Emails

Managing your inbox is key to staying organized. Gmail (and most email apps) offer several features to keep your emails sorted:

Folders and Labels

1. **Labels**: Gmail uses labels (instead of folders) to organize emails. You can create custom labels to sort emails by category (e.g., "Work," "Important," etc.). To create a new label, tap the **three dots** in the top-right corner of an open email, select **Label**, and choose or create a new label.
2. **Folders**: In the **Email app**, you can create folders to organize emails manually. Tap **Settings > Folders > Create new folder** to organize your emails.

Tip: Use labels or folders to keep your inbox clutter-free and make it easier to find important emails.

Archiving Emails

If you want to remove emails from your inbox without deleting them:

1. Open the email you want to archive.

2. Tap the **Archive** icon (usually a **box** with a downward arrow).
3. The email will be moved to the **All Mail** folder, keeping it out of your inbox but accessible later.

Tip: Archiving emails helps keep your inbox neat while preserving them for future reference.

Searching for Emails

If you're looking for a specific email, the **search feature** in your email app is super helpful:

1. Open the **Gmail** or **Email app**.
2. Tap the **search bar** at the top.
3. Type keywords, contact names, or phrases to find the email you're looking for.

Tip: You can use advanced search options in Gmail, like "from:", "to:", or "subject:" to narrow down your search.

Managing Email Notifications

You can control how and when you get notifications for new emails:

1. Open the **Gmail app**.
2. Tap the **three-line menu** icon > **Settings**.
3. Tap the account you want to manage notifications for.
4. Under **Notifications**, choose your preferred option:

- **All**: Get notified for every email.

- **High priority only**: Only get notified for important emails.
- **None**: Turn off all notifications.

*Pro Tip: If you want to mute certain email threads that are too busy, open the thread, tap the **three dots** > **Mute**.*

Adding and Removing Email Accounts

If you want to add or remove an email account:

To Add an Account:

1. Open the **Gmail** or **Email app**.
2. Tap the **three-line menu** icon > **Settings**.
3. Tap **Add account** and follow the prompts for the account you want to add.

To Remove an Account:

1. Go to **Settings** in the Gmail app.
2. Tap the account you want to remove.
3. Scroll down and tap **Remove account**.

Tip: Removing an account from your phone won't delete the email account itself; it only removes it from the device.

8. Setting Up and Using Email on Other Apps (Outlook, Yahoo, etc.)

If you prefer using apps like **Outlook** or **Yahoo Mail**, you can download these apps from the Google Play Store and follow their setup instructions, similar to how you set up Gmail.

Most of these apps support multiple email accounts and sync with services like Google, Outlook, Yahoo, and others.

Chapter 7

Connecting to the Internet and Bluetooth

Your Moto G Stylus 5G is designed to keep you connected to the internet and other devices seamlessly. Whether you're using Wi-Fi, mobile data, or Bluetooth, this chapter will guide you through the steps for setting up and managing your connections.

Wi-Fi Setup and Management

Wi-Fi allows you to access the internet without using mobile data. Here's how to connect your Moto G Stylus 5G to a Wi-Fi network:

Connecting to a Wi-Fi Network

1. **Open the Settings app**.
2. Tap **Network & Internet** > **Wi-Fi**.
3. Toggle the Wi-Fi switch to **On**. Your device will start scanning for available networks.
4. Choose your desired Wi-Fi network from the list of available options.
5. **Enter the Wi-Fi password** (if required) and tap **Connect**.

Pro Tip: To save battery, you can turn off Wi-Fi when you're not using it. Your phone will automatically reconnect to saved networks when you're within range.

Managing Wi-Fi Networks

- **Forget a Network**: If you no longer wish to automatically connect to a network, tap the **gear icon** next to the network name and select **Forget**.
- **Manage Network Settings**: You can configure advanced Wi-Fi settings by tapping the **gear icon** next to the network, such as static IP or proxy settings.

Tip: For security, always connect to networks that require a password, and avoid using unsecured public networks for sensitive activities.

Using Mobile Data

Mobile data allows you to access the internet when Wi-Fi is not available. Here's how to set up and manage mobile data:

Turning Mobile Data On or Off

1. Open the **Settings app**.
2. Tap **Network & Internet > Mobile network**.
3. Toggle **Mobile data** to **On** to begin using your carrier's mobile data.
4. To turn it off, simply toggle **Mobile data** to **Off**.

*Tip: You can quickly turn mobile data on or off from the **Quick Settings** menu by swiping down from the top of the screen and tapping the **Mobile data** icon.*

- **Data Saver**: If you want to limit your data usage, turn on **Data Saver**. This feature restricts background data usage by apps.
    1. Go to **Settings** > **Network & Internet** > **Data Saver**.
    2. Toggle **Data Saver** to **On** to enable it.
- **Set Data Usage Limits**: You can set a data usage warning and limit to avoid exceeding your data plan.
    1. Go to **Settings** > **Network & Internet** > **Data usage**.
    2. Set your data usage limits to get notified when you're nearing your data cap.

 Pro Tip: When you're traveling internationally, consider using data roaming options or buying a local SIM card to save on data costs.

Pairing with Bluetooth Devices

Bluetooth allows you to wirelessly connect your Moto G Stylus 5G to various devices like headphones, speakers, smartwatches, and more. Here's how to set up Bluetooth connections:

Turning On Bluetooth

1. Open the **Settings app**.
2. Tap **Connected devices** > **Bluetooth**.
3. Toggle the Bluetooth switch to **On**. Your device will start scanning for nearby Bluetooth devices.

1. Once Bluetooth is on, your phone will display a list of available devices. Tap the device you want to connect to.
2. If prompted, **enter a PIN or confirm the pairing** on both devices. Some devices may require you to tap **Pair** or **Accept** on both the phone and the Bluetooth device.
3. Once connected, your phone will display a message confirming the connection.

 *Tip: You can also pair Bluetooth headphones or speakers directly from the **Quick Settings** menu by tapping the **Bluetooth icon** and selecting the device you want to connect to.*

Managing Paired Devices

- To manage paired Bluetooth devices, go to **Settings** > **Connected devices** > **Bluetooth**. Tap a device's name to disconnect, forget, or adjust settings.
- **Forget a Device**: If you no longer want to stay connected to a device, tap the **gear icon** next to the device name and select **Forget**.

Troubleshooting Connectivity Issues

If you're having trouble connecting to Wi-Fi, mobile data, or Bluetooth, here are some troubleshooting tips:

Wi-Fi Troubleshooting

- Make sure you're within range of the Wi-Fi network and that it is working properly.
- If the connection is slow or unstable, try restarting your router and your phone.
- Ensure that you've entered the correct password.
- Toggle **Airplane mode** on and off, which can help reset connections.

Mobile Data Troubleshooting

- Make sure mobile data is enabled in your settings.
- Check if you've reached your data limit by reviewing your mobile carrier settings.
- Restart your phone to refresh your connection to the mobile network.
- Verify that **Airplane mode** is off and mobile data is turned on.

Bluetooth Troubleshooting

- Ensure the Bluetooth device you're trying to pair is powered on and in pairing mode.
- If the device doesn't appear in the list, try turning Bluetooth off and back on again.
- Restart your phone and the Bluetooth device.
- Move closer to the Bluetooth device to ensure the connection is within range.

The Moto G Stylus 5G is equipped with an impressive camera that allows you to capture high-quality photos and videos. This chapter will show you how to use the camera effectively, from exploring its features to editing and sharing your media.

Camera Modes and Features

The Moto G Stylus 5G camera offers various modes and features that make it easy to capture stunning shots in different situations. Here's an overview of the most important modes and settings:

Basic Camera Modes

1. **Photo Mode**: This is the default mode for capturing still images. The camera will automatically adjust for focus, exposure, and lighting conditions.
2. **Video Mode**: Switch to video mode to record high-definition videos. You can easily switch between photos and videos by swiping the shutter button.
3. **Portrait Mode**: Use this mode to capture portraits with a beautiful background blur (bokeh effect), which makes your subject stand out.
4. **Night Vision Mode**: This mode enhances low-light performance by brightening your photos and reducing noise for clear shots in the dark.
5. **Pro Mode**: Take control of the camera settings like ISO, shutter speed, focus, and white balance for a more hands-on, manual experience. This is ideal for users who want full creative control over their photos.

6. **Ultra-Wide Mode**: This mode uses the ultra-wide camera lens to capture a broader view, perfect for group shots or landscapes.
7. **Macro Mode**: Get up close to your subject and capture detailed shots with the macro lens for crisp and sharp images of tiny objects.
8. **Panorama Mode**: Capture wide-angle shots, such as scenic landscapes or large groups, by slowly panning the camera from left to right.
9. **Slow Motion Mode**: Record videos at a higher frame rate to create slow-motion effects.
10. **Time-Lapse Mode**: Capture time-lapse videos, speeding up the scene to showcase long-term processes like sunset or traffic flow.

Camera Settings

To adjust the camera settings:

1. Open the **Camera app**.
2. Tap the **gear icon** (Settings) in the top-left corner to customize camera options like:

- **Grid Lines**: Helps you follow the rule of thirds for better composition.
- **Shutter Sound**: Turn off the camera shutter sound if needed.
- **Video Resolution**: Adjust the resolution of your video recording (e.g., 1080p, 4K).

Taking Photos and Videos

Now that you know about the camera modes, here's how to take great photos and videos on your Moto G Stylus 5G:

1. Open the **Camera app**.
2. Select **Photo Mode** (the default mode).
3. Tap anywhere on the screen to focus on your subject. The camera will automatically adjust the exposure.
4. Press the **shutter button** (the round white button) to take a photo.
5. You can tap the **flash icon** (lightning bolt) to enable or disable the flash.
6. Use the **volume buttons** to take a photo if you prefer physical controls (this is especially useful for selfies).

*Pro Tip: For clearer photos, keep your hands steady when pressing the shutter button, or use the camera's **auto-stabilization** feature for added stability.*

Taking Videos

1. Open the **Camera app** and swipe left or right to switch to **Video Mode**.
2. Tap the **shutter button** to start recording.
3. While recording, you can tap the screen to focus on specific objects.
4. Tap the **shutter button** again to stop recording.
5. Adjust the **zoom slider** to zoom in or out during the recording.

Pro Tip: To ensure steady video recording, consider using a tripod or a gimbal if you plan to film for extended periods.

Editing and Sharing Media

Once you've captured your perfect photo or video, you can use the built-in editing tools to enhance your media before sharing it with others.

Editing Photos

1. Open the **Gallery app** and select the photo you want to edit.
2. Tap the **edit icon** (pencil icon) to enter the photo editor.
3. Use the available editing tools, such as:

- **Crop**: Trim the edges of your photo to focus on the main subject.
- **Filters**: Apply various color and effect filters to change the look of your photo.
- **Adjust**: Modify brightness, contrast, saturation, and sharpness for a more polished result.
- **Text and Draw**: Add text or doodles to your image using the available drawing tools.
- **Healing Tool**: Remove blemishes or unwanted objects from your photo.

*Pro Tip: Use the **undo** button to reverse any changes you don't like and experiment with different filters to find your favorite look.*

Editing Videos

1. Open the **Gallery app** and select the video you want to edit.

2. Tap the **edit icon** (scissors icon) to enter the video editor.
3. Trim the beginning or end of the video, or use the **split** tool to cut the video into segments.
4. You can also apply filters, adjust the video speed (for slow motion or time-lapse), and add background music or sound effects.

Tip: When editing video, consider adding music or sound effects to enhance the viewing experience, especially for social media posts.

Sharing Photos and Videos

Once you've edited your photos and videos, you can easily share them through various apps and platforms. Here's how:

1. Open the **Gallery app** and select the photo or video you want to share.
2. Tap the **share icon** (three dots connected by lines) to open the sharing options.
3. Choose the app or service you want to share with (e.g., WhatsApp, Instagram, Facebook, or email).
4. Select the recipient and add a message if necessary, then tap **Send**.

Chapter 9

Organizing Your Photos and Videos

With the Moto G Stylus 5G, organizing your photos and videos is easier than ever. Whether you're keeping track of memories or managing your media collection, this chapter will guide you through using **Google Photos** to organize, create albums, and back up your content to the cloud.

Using Google Photos

Google Photos is the default app for organizing, editing, and backing up your media on Android devices. Here's how to use it effectively:

Opening Google Photos

1. Open the **Google Photos app** from your apps drawer or home screen.
2. The app will automatically display all the photos and videos stored on your device in a chronological timeline.

- **Photos Tab**: Displays all your photos and videos in the order they were taken.
- **Albums Tab**: Organizes your media into albums, automatically grouping photos by people, places, and events.
- **Search Tab**: Allows you to search for specific photos by people, places, or objects within your media library. You can search by typing terms like "beach" or "dog," and Google Photos will display relevant photos.

*Tip: You can also use **face recognition** in Google Photos to quickly find photos of specific people, if the feature is enabled.*

Editing Photos in Google Photos

1. Select the photo you want to edit.
2. Tap the **edit icon** (pencil icon) to enter the photo editor.
3. You can crop, adjust brightness, contrast, and more. Google Photos also offers automatic enhancements with a **magic wand** icon for one-tap edits.
4. Once done, tap **Save** to apply changes.

*Pro Tip: Google Photos offers a **live photos** feature, which can turn any still image into a short video, capturing a brief moment before and after you take the picture.*

Creating Albums and Slideshows

Organizing your media into albums or creating slideshows is a great way to keep your photos and videos accessible. Here's how:

Creating Albums

1. Open the **Google Photos app**.
2. Tap the **Library** tab at the bottom.
3. Tap **Albums > Create album**.
4. Enter a name for your album and tap **Select photos**.
5. Choose the photos and videos you want to add to the album, then tap **Done**.
6. To add more media to the album later, tap the album and select **Add photos**.

 Tip: You can create albums based on events, trips, or themes like "Family," "Vacation," or "Work."

Creating Slideshows

1. Open the **Google Photos app** and navigate to an album or collection of photos.
2. Tap the **three-dot menu** in the top-right corner.
3. Select **Slideshow** from the options. The app will play the photos in the album as a slideshow.

Tip: For a more dynamic slideshow, you can also use apps like Google Slides or third-party slideshow apps to add music or transitions.

Backing Up Media to the Cloud

One of the main advantages of using Google Photos is the ability to back up your photos and videos to the cloud, ensuring your media is safe and accessible from any device.

Turning On Backup and Sync

1. Open the **Google Photos app**.
2. Tap your **profile icon** in the top-right corner and select **Photos settings**.
3. Tap **Back up & sync**.
4. Toggle **Back up & sync** to **On**.
5. Choose whether you want to back up photos using **High quality** (free, unlimited storage) or **Original quality** (counts against your Google storage quota).
6. You can also choose whether to back up photos over **Wi-Fi** only or also use mobile data.

*Tip: If you have limited storage on your Google account, you might want to use **High quality** to save space. If you prefer original resolution, be mindful of your storage limits.*

Managing Your Google Storage

Google provides 15GB of free storage across all its services, including Gmail, Google Photos, and Google Drive. Here's how to manage it:

1. Open the **Google Photos app**.
2. Tap your **profile icon** and select **Google Photos settings**.

3. Tap **Manage storage** to see how much space you've used and whether you need to free up space or upgrade to Google One for more storage.

Tip: If you're running low on storage, you can delete old photos and videos you no longer need, or upgrade to **Google One** *for additional cloud storage.*

Accessing Media from Other Devices

Since your photos are stored in the cloud, you can access them on any device with the Google Photos app or via the **Google Photos website** (photos.google.com). Simply log in with your Google account to view, edit, and share your media.

Freeing Up Space on Your Device

Once your photos and videos are backed up to the cloud, you can choose to delete them from your device to free up space. Here's how:

1. Open the **Google Photos app**.
2. Tap your **profile icon** and select **Free up space**.
3. Google Photos will suggest photos and videos that have already been backed up. You can tap **Free up** to delete these from your device.
4. You can also choose to keep certain photos or videos if needed.

The Moto G Stylus 5G comes preloaded with a range of essential apps that can help you stay organized, productive, and entertained. This chapter will guide you through using key apps like **Calendar, Clock, Calculator, Files, Google Drive**, and the **Play Store** to download more apps.

Calendar, Clock, and Calculator

These basic apps are essential for managing your schedule, keeping track of time, and performing simple calculations.

Using the Calendar App

The **Google Calendar** app helps you manage your schedule and set reminders for important events. Here's how to use it:

1. Open the **Calendar app** from your apps drawer or home screen.
2. Tap the **+** button to create a new event.
3. Fill in the event details, such as the **title**, **date**, **time**, and **location**.
4. You can also set a reminder or repeat settings for recurring events.
5. Tap **Save** to add the event to your calendar.

Tip: Sync your calendar with your Google account to access your events across all your devices.

The **Clock app** helps you keep track of time and set alarms. Here's how to use it:

1. Open the **Clock app** from your apps drawer or home screen.
2. **Set an Alarm**: Tap the **alarm icon** and then the **+** button to add a new alarm. Set the desired time and sound.
3. **Use the Stopwatch**: Tap the **stopwatch icon** to start timing an event.
4. **Use the Timer**: Tap the **timer icon** to set a countdown timer for cooking, workouts, or any other timed activity.

 Pro Tip: You can also use the Clock app's **World Clock** feature to check the time in other locations around the world.

Using the Calculator App

The **Calculator app** is a simple tool for performing basic math calculations:

1. Open the **Calculator app**.
2. Use the on-screen buttons to perform arithmetic calculations like addition, subtraction, multiplication, and division.
3. For more advanced calculations, rotate your phone to switch to the **scientific calculator** mode, which offers functions like sine, cosine, and square roots.

Files and Google Drive

These apps help you manage, organize, and back up your files.

Using the Files App

The **Files app** is your file manager, allowing you to browse and organize documents, photos, videos, and more. Here's how to use it:

1. Open the **Files app** from your apps drawer or home screen.
2. Browse through your **Internal storage** or **SD card** to view and manage your files.
3. You can **create folders** to organize your files by tapping the **three-dot menu** and selecting **Create folder**.
4. To move or delete files, tap and hold on a file to select it, then use the options in the bottom menu.

Tip: The Files app also lets you search for specific files by name, file type, or date.

Using Google Drive

Google Drive is a cloud-based storage service that lets you store, share, and access files from anywhere. Here's how to use it:

1. Open the **Google Drive app** from your apps drawer or home screen.

2. To upload files to Google Drive, tap the **+** button and choose **Upload**. Select the files or folders from your device to upload.
3. To create new documents, sheets, slides, or forms, tap the **+** button and select the type of file you want to create.
4. You can also share files with others by right-clicking on a file and selecting **Share**, then entering the email addresses of people you want to share with.

*Pro Tip: Google Drive gives you 15GB of free storage across all Google services, which you can expand by upgrading to **Google One**.*

Using Play Store to Download Apps

The **Google Play Store** is where you can find a wide range of apps, games, and media to enhance your Moto G Stylus 5G experience. Here's how to explore and download apps:

Browsing and Searching for Apps

1. Open the **Google Play Store** app from your apps drawer.
2. Browse the **Home** page to find featured apps, games, or categories like **Top Charts**, **Trending**, and more.
3. To search for a specific app, tap the **search bar** at the top and type in the name or category of the app you're looking for.

1. Once you've found an app you want, tap on its listing.
2. Tap **Install** to begin downloading the app to your device.
3. Once the app is installed, you can open it directly from the Play Store or from your apps drawer.

*Tip: If you've already installed an app, the button will say **Open** instead of **Install**, allowing you to launch the app directly from the Play Store.*

Managing Your Apps

You can easily manage your apps from the **Play Store**:

1. Open the **Play Store** app.
2. Tap your **profile icon** in the top-right corner and select **My apps & games**.
3. Here, you can see apps that need updating, as well as the ones you've installed.

Chapter 11

Using Google Assistant and Voice Commands

Google Assistant is a powerful tool that allows you to interact with your Moto G Stylus 5G hands-free, making it easier to perform tasks and get information. This chapter will guide you through activating and using Google Assistant, as well as utilizing voice commands for everyday tasks.

1. Activating Google Assistant

Google Assistant is built into your Moto G Stylus 5G, and you can activate it using voice commands or gestures.

Voice Activation

To activate Google Assistant by voice, simply say **"Hey Google"** or **"Ok Google."** Your phone will respond with a beep, and the Assistant will be ready to help.

Gesture Activation

If you prefer not to use your voice, you can activate Google Assistant using gestures:

1. **Swipe Up from the Bottom**: Swipe up from the bottom of the screen and hold to open Google Assistant.
2. **Press the Home Button**: On certain devices, you can press and hold the **home button** to activate Google Assistant.

*Pro Tip: Make sure **Voice Match** is enabled in your Google Assistant settings to ensure it recognizes your voice and responds when you say "Hey Google."*

Using the Google Assistant Button

Some Moto G Stylus 5G devices may have a dedicated button or shortcut for Google Assistant. Check your settings to see if this feature is enabled.

2. Useful Commands for Everyday Tasks

Google Assistant is capable of performing a wide range of tasks, from setting reminders to controlling your smart home devices. Here are some of the most useful voice commands for everyday tasks:

General Commands

- **"What's the weather like today?"**: Get a weather forecast for your location.
- **"What time is it in [city]?"**: Ask for the time in a different time zone.
- **"What's the traffic like?"**: Check traffic conditions for your commute.
- **"Set an alarm for [time]."**: Set a one-time alarm.

67

- **"Set a reminder to [task] at [time]."**: Get a reminder for a specific task at a chosen time.

Navigation and Maps

- **"Navigate to [address or place]."**: Get directions to your destination.
- **"How long will it take to get to [location]?"**: Ask for an estimated travel time to your location.
- **"Find restaurants near me."**: Discover nearby dining options.

Calls and Messages

- **"Call [contact name]."**: Make a phone call to a saved contact.
- **"Send a text to [contact name] saying [message]."**: Send an SMS or MMS to a contact.
- **"Send an email to [contact name]."**: Compose and send an email.

Entertainment

- **"Play [song/artist/playlist] on [music app]."**: Listen to music on your preferred streaming service.
- **"Show me funny cat videos."**: Ask for a specific type of content on YouTube or other services.
- **"What's the latest news?"**: Get news updates from a variety of sources.

Smart Home Control

If you have smart home devices connected, you can use Google Assistant to control them:

- **"Turn off the lights."**: Turn off compatible smart lights.
- **"Adjust the thermostat to [temperature]."**: Control your smart thermostat.

*Tip: Customize your Google Assistant to recognize your voice and personal preferences for a smoother experience. This is done through the **Assistant settings**.*

3. Voice Typing and Hands-Free Use

Google Assistant not only performs tasks, but it also allows you to use voice commands for hands-free typing and other functions, making your device more accessible.

Using Voice Typing

One of the most convenient features of Google Assistant is the ability to dictate text instead of typing. Here's how to use voice typing:

1. In any text field (e.g., composing a message or note), tap the **microphone icon** on the keyboard.
2. Start speaking, and Google Assistant will transcribe your words into text.
3. Once you're done, tap **send**, **done**, or **enter** to complete the action.

Tip: Speak clearly and at a steady pace for the best transcription accuracy. You can also use punctuation commands like "comma," "period," or "question mark."

With Google Assistant, you can control many aspects of your device without touching it. This is especially useful when you're driving, cooking, or performing other tasks where your hands are busy.

1. **Voice Commands for Apps**: You can launch apps with commands like:

- "Open [app name]."
- "Play [song/playlist] on [music app]."

2. **Hands-Free Control of Settings**: Adjust settings such as:

- "Turn on Do Not Disturb."
- "Turn on Bluetooth."
- "Increase the brightness."

3. **Dictating Messages or Notes**: Dictate text messages, reminders, and notes without touching your phone.

- **"Create a note that says [note content]."**
- **"Send a text to [contact name] saying [message]."**

Chapter 12

Battery Life and Power Management

Maximizing your battery life is crucial for getting the most out of your Moto G Stylus 5G. This chapter will guide you through checking your battery usage, tips for extending battery life, and the charging options available to you, including fast charging.

Checking Battery Usage

Understanding how your battery is being used is the first step toward managing its life effectively. The Moto G Stylus 5G provides an easy way to monitor your battery consumption.

Checking Battery Usage in Settings

1. Open the **Settings** app from your apps drawer or home screen.
2. Scroll down and tap on **Battery**.
3. Here, you'll see an overview of your battery usage, including:

- **Battery percentage**: Displays how much charge is remaining.

- **Screen usage**: Shows how much power is being consumed by the display.
- **App usage**: Lists the apps consuming the most battery, allowing you to identify and manage power-hungry apps.

4. You can tap on **Battery usage** to get a more detailed breakdown of your usage over the past 24 hours or 7 days.

Tip: If you notice certain apps consuming excessive battery, consider limiting background activity or uninstalling them if not necessary.

Tips to Extend Battery Life

The Moto G Stylus 5G comes with several built-in features to help conserve battery life, along with practical tips to make your device last longer on a single charge.

Optimize Battery Settings

1. **Enable Battery Saver**:

- Go to **Settings** > **Battery** > **Battery Saver**.
- Turn on **Battery Saver** to reduce background activity and limit app performance.
- You can also set **Battery Saver** to activate automatically when your battery reaches a certain percentage (e.g., 15%).

2. **Use Adaptive Battery**:

- In **Settings** > **Battery**, enable **Adaptive Battery**. This feature uses machine learning to identify apps you don't use often and limits their background activity.

3. **Disable Battery-Draining Features**:

- **Location Services**: Turn off location services when you don't need them. Go to **Settings** > **Location** and toggle it off.
- **Bluetooth and Wi-Fi**: Turn off Bluetooth and Wi-Fi when not in use. You can use the **Quick Settings** menu to disable these features.
- **Vibration**: Use regular ringtones instead of vibration to save power. Go to **Settings** > **Sound** > **Vibrate** and disable unnecessary vibrations.

4. **Adjust Screen Brightness**:

- Go to **Settings** > **Display** > **Brightness level** and adjust it to a lower setting.
- You can also enable **Adaptive brightness**, which automatically adjusts the screen brightness based on your surroundings.

5. **Limit Background Apps**:

- Close apps running in the background that you aren't actively using. To see running apps, go to the **Overview** screen by tapping the square button and swipe away apps you no longer need.

6. **Enable Dark Mode**:

- Dark Mode uses less power on OLED screens by reducing the brightness of your display. To enable it, go to **Settings** > **Display** > **Dark theme**.

*Tip: Turning on **Airplane Mode** when you don't need network connectivity (like during flights) can significantly save battery power.*

Charging and Fast Charging Options

Charging your Moto G Stylus 5G efficiently ensures you don't spend more time plugged in than necessary. Here's everything you need to know about charging your device and using fast charging options.

Charging Your Phone

1. **Using the Charger in the Box**: Your Moto G Stylus 5G comes with a fast-charging adapter and USB-C cable. To charge your phone, plug the cable into the phone and adapter, then plug the adapter into an electrical outlet. Charging time varies depending on battery level, but it typically takes around 1.5 to 2 hours to fully charge the device.
2. **Using Wireless Charging**: While the Moto G Stylus 5G supports wireless charging, it is not as fast as wired charging. Simply place your device on a **Qi-compatible wireless charging pad** to charge it without plugging in a cable.

Fast Charging

The Moto G Stylus 5G supports **TurboPower** fast charging, which can charge your phone quickly when you're in a hurry. Here's how to take advantage of it:

1. **TurboPower Charging**: To benefit from TurboPower, use the **included charger** or a compatible **18W+ USB-C charger**. The Moto G Stylus 5G can charge up to 50% in about 30 minutes with TurboPower charging.
2. **Charging Tips**:

   - Always use the provided charging cable and adapter for the fastest charge.
   - If you use a third-party charger, make sure it's compatible with fast charging (18W or higher).
   - Avoid charging your phone while using high-performance apps or playing games, as this can slow down the charging process.

Wireless Charging Pads and Power Banks

If you prefer wireless charging, use a **Qi-certified wireless charging pad**. Wireless charging pads may charge slower than wired charging but offer the convenience of no cables.

You can also use a **power bank** for charging on the go. Ensure the power bank supports fast charging if you want quicker results.

Chapter 13

Security and Privacy Settings

Keeping your Moto G Stylus 5G secure and protecting your personal information is essential. This chapter will guide you through setting up fingerprint and face unlock, choosing the right screen lock method, and managing app permissions to enhance your device's security and privacy.

Fingerprint and Face Unlock

The Moto G Stylus 5G offers convenient biometric options for unlocking your device: **Fingerprint unlock** and **Face unlock**. These features provide secure access to your phone while reducing the need for manual entry of a PIN or password.

Setting Up Fingerprint Unlock

To enable fingerprint unlock, follow these steps:

1. Go to **Settings** > **Security** > **Fingerprint**.
2. Tap **Add fingerprint** and follow the on-screen instructions. You'll be prompted to place your finger on the fingerprint sensor located on the back of the

device or, in some cases, integrated into the power button.
3. Make sure to register multiple fingerprints (e.g., both thumbs or your index fingers) for easier access.

Tip: To ensure optimal recognition, keep your finger clean and dry while registering.

Setting Up Face Unlock

To enable face unlock, follow these steps:

1. Go to **Settings** > **Security** > **Face recognition**.
2. Tap **Set up face recognition** and follow the on-screen instructions to align your face with the camera.
3. After setup, you can use face unlock to quickly access your phone.

Tip: Face unlock may not work well in low-light conditions, so make sure the room is sufficiently lit for optimal performance.

Setting a Screen Lock

In addition to biometric unlock methods, you should set up a screen lock for additional security. The Moto G Stylus 5G offers several lock screen options to suit your preferences.

Setting Up a PIN, Pattern, or Password

1. Go to **Settings** > **Security** > **Screen lock**.
2. Choose between **Pattern**, **PIN**, or **Password** as your screen lock type:

- **Pattern**: Draw a unique pattern on the screen to unlock your device.
- **PIN**: Enter a 4-6 digit number to unlock your phone.
- **Password**: Set a more complex alphanumeric password for extra security.

3. Once you've selected your preferred lock type, follow the on-screen prompts to set up your chosen lock screen method.

Pro Tip: A password offers the highest level of security, but a PIN or pattern is quicker to enter. Choose one based on your needs.

Lock Screen Notifications

You can also adjust what appears on your lock screen:

1. Go to **Settings** > **Display** > **Lock screen**.
2. Here, you can choose whether you want to show notifications, widgets, or none at all while the device is locked.

Tip: To prevent private information from showing on your lock screen, you can hide sensitive content in notifications.

Managing App Permissions

Your apps have access to various features of your phone, like the camera, microphone, and location services. It's important to review and manage these permissions to protect your privacy.

1. Go to **Settings** > **Apps** > **See all apps**.
2. Tap on the app you want to manage permissions for.
3. Select **Permissions** to view which permissions the app has and toggle them on or off as needed. You can control access to:

   - Camera
   - Microphone
   - Location
   - Contacts
   - Storage

Tip: Only grant permissions that are essential for the app's functionality. For example, a weather app may need access to your location, but a flashlight app does not.

Granting Permissions for New Apps

When you install a new app, you'll typically be prompted to grant permissions. Before granting permissions:

1. Read the request carefully to ensure the app needs the permissions it's asking for.
2. You can deny permissions and still use some features of the app, depending on what it requires.

Using Permission Manager for More Control

1. Go to **Settings** > **Privacy** > **Permission manager**.
2. Here, you can view all app permissions by category (e.g., Location, Camera, Microphone) and see which apps have access to each feature.

3. You can then adjust individual app permissions based on your preferences.

Chapter 14

Accessibility Features for Seniors

The Moto G Stylus 5G includes a variety of accessibility features designed to make the device easier to use for individuals with different needs, including seniors. This chapter will walk you through how to enlarge text and adjust display settings, use high contrast and color options, and enable features like TalkBack and Magnification for better usability.

Enlarging Text and Display Size

If the text on your Moto G Stylus 5G is too small or hard to read, you can easily enlarge it for better visibility.

Enlarging Text

To make text larger across all apps and menus:

1. Go to **Settings** > **Accessibility** > **Font size**.
2. Use the slider to increase or decrease the font size to your preferred level. The larger the slider, the larger the text will appear.

📝 Tip: Enlarge the text for better readability in email, messages, and other apps.

Adjusting Display Size

To make everything on your screen larger, including icons and buttons:

1. Go to **Settings** > **Accessibility** > **Display size**.
2. Use the slider to adjust the display size. Increasing the size will make all elements on the screen, including icons and text, larger and easier to read.

Pro Tip: Adjust both font size and display size for maximum readability. These settings will make the overall user interface more senior-friendly.

High Contrast and Color Options

For seniors with visual impairments or those who prefer enhanced visibility, the Moto G Stylus 5G offers options to improve screen contrast and color settings.

High Contrast Text

To make text easier to read by increasing contrast:

1. Go to **Settings** > **Accessibility** > **High contrast text**.
2. Turn on the toggle to enable high contrast text. This will make the text appear bolder and stand out against the background, improving readability.

If you or someone you know has difficulty distinguishing certain colors, you can adjust the color settings:

1. Go to **Settings** > **Accessibility** > **Color correction**.
2. Turn on **Color correction** and select the color adjustment mode that works best (e.g., **Deuteranomaly**, **Protanomaly**, or **Tritanomaly**) for specific types of colorblindness.

Invert Colors for Enhanced Contrast

If the contrast still isn't enough, you can invert the colors on your device to make reading easier:

1. Go to **Settings** > **Accessibility** > **Display**.
2. Enable **Invert colors** to turn the screen's colors upside down, with white turning black and vice versa.

Tip: Inverting colors and enabling high contrast text together can significantly improve visibility for users with low vision.

Using TalkBack and Magnification

These features are designed to assist seniors who may have trouble reading text or seeing small details on the screen.

TalkBack is an accessibility feature that reads aloud the text displayed on the screen, helping visually impaired users navigate their phone.

1. Go to **Settings > Accessibility > TalkBack**.
2. Toggle on **TalkBack** to activate it. Once activated, TalkBack will read aloud whatever is selected on the screen.
3. To navigate, swipe with two fingers, and TalkBack will guide you through actions like opening apps, reading messages, and more.
4. You can customize the speech settings and gesture shortcuts for more personalized control.

Tip: TalkBack works best when you are using gestures, such as swiping with two fingers to scroll or tapping with one finger to select items. Practice these gestures for a smooth experience.

Magnification Gestures: Zoom In for Better Visibility

Magnification gestures allow you to zoom in on any part of the screen to see details more clearly.

1. Go to **Settings > Accessibility > Magnification**.
2. Turn on **Magnification gestures**.
3. To use magnification, tap the screen three times quickly to zoom in. Drag two fingers to move around the zoomed-in screen.
4. To zoom out, tap three times again.

Pro Tip: You can adjust the zoom level and activate magnification quickly by triple-tapping anywhere on the screen.

Chapter 15

Storage and File Management

Properly managing storage on your Moto G Stylus 5G is essential for maintaining performance and ensuring you have enough space for your important files and apps. This chapter will guide you through checking available storage, moving files to an SD card, and cleaning up unused apps and files to optimize your device.

Checking Available Storage

Before managing your storage, it's helpful to first check how much space you have left on your device.

Viewing Storage Usage

1. Go to **Settings** > **Storage**.
2. The storage screen will display an overview of your available and used space, including:

- **Total storage**: The total capacity of your device.
- **Used storage**: The amount of space already occupied by apps, media, and system files.
- **Free storage**: The remaining available space.

3. Tap on **Used storage** to see a detailed breakdown of storage usage by category:

- **Apps**: How much space is used by apps and their data.
- **Photos and Videos**: Space taken by your media files.
- **Audio**: Space used by music and other audio files.
- **Downloads**: Files saved from the internet or email attachments.
- **System**: Space used by system files and updates.

Tip: If you're running low on space, check which apps or files are taking up the most room to determine what to remove or move.

Moving Files to SD Card

If you have a microSD card installed in your Moto G Stylus 5G, you can move photos, videos, and some apps to the SD card to free up space on your internal storage.

Moving Media Files (Photos, Videos, Music) to SD Card

1. Open the **Files** app or use a file manager.
2. Navigate to the **Internal storage** section and find the files you want to move.
3. Select the files (photos, videos, or music), then tap the **three-dot menu** in the top-right corner and choose **Move** or **Copy**.
4. Select the **SD Card** as the destination and choose the folder where you want to store the files.
5. Tap **Move here** or **Copy here** to complete the process.

Moving Apps to SD Card

Some apps can be moved to an SD card to free up space in internal storage, though not all apps support this feature.

1. Go to **Settings** > **Apps**.
2. Tap on the app you want to move.
3. Select **Storage**.
4. If the app supports it, you'll see an option to **Change** storage location. Tap on it and select **SD card**.
5. Tap **Move** to transfer the app to the SD card.

Note: Some apps, especially system apps and larger apps with live data, might not be able to be moved to the SD card.

Cleaning Up Unused Apps and Files

Over time, you may accumulate unused apps, old files, and cached data that can take up valuable storage. Cleaning up these files can help optimize your device's performance.

Uninstalling Unused Apps

1. Go to **Settings** > **Apps** > **See all apps**.
2. Browse through the list and identify apps you no longer use.
3. Tap on an app and select **Uninstall**.
4. Confirm the uninstallation when prompted.

*Tip: You can also go to the **Play Store** > **My apps & games** and uninstall apps directly from the "Installed" section.*

Clearing App Cache and Data

Apps accumulate cache data that can sometimes take up a lot of space. You can clear this cache to recover some storage.

1. Go to **Settings** > **Apps** > **See all apps**.
2. Select the app you want to clear the cache for.
3. Tap on **Storage**.
4. Select **Clear Cache** to remove temporary data that is stored by the app.

Warning: Clearing an app's data will remove any saved information like login credentials or settings, so use it carefully.

Using the "Free Up Space" Tool

The Moto G Stylus 5G includes a built-in tool to help you easily clean up unused files.

1. Go to **Settings** > **Storage**.
2. Tap **Free up space** to see a list of files that are safe to delete, such as:

- **Downloaded files**: Documents, PDFs, and other files from the internet.
- **Old photos and videos**: Images and videos that haven't been viewed in a long time.
- **Unused apps**: Apps that you haven't opened in a while.

3. Select the files you want to delete, then tap **Delete**.

Chapter 16

Troubleshooting Common Issues

While using your Moto G Stylus 5G, you may encounter some common issues. This chapter will help you troubleshoot and resolve problems such as your phone not turning on, Wi-Fi or network problems, and app crashes or freezing.

Phone Not Turning On

If your Moto G Stylus 5G isn't turning on, follow these steps to troubleshoot the issue:

Check the Battery

1. **Charge your device**: Connect your phone to a charger and let it charge for at least 15-30 minutes. If the battery was completely drained, it may take a little time before the phone responds.
2. **Try a different charger**: If charging doesn't work, try using a different charger or charging cable, as the current one might be faulty.
3. **Check for charging port issues**: Inspect the charging port for dirt or debris that may prevent the charging cable from connecting properly.

If the phone seems to be unresponsive, try a forced restart:

1. Press and hold the **Power button** and the **Volume Down button** simultaneously for about 10-15 seconds.
2. Your phone should vibrate and reboot, which may resolve the issue.

Perform a Recovery Mode Reset (if still not turning on)

1. With the phone powered off, press and hold the **Volume Down** and **Power** buttons together until the device vibrates.
2. You will enter **Recovery Mode**. Use the volume buttons to navigate to **Wipe Cache Partition** and press the power button to select it.
3. After the process completes, select **Reboot system now**.

If the phone still won't turn on, contact customer support or visit a service center for further assistance.

Wi-Fi or Network Problems

If you're experiencing issues with Wi-Fi or mobile network connectivity, try the following troubleshooting steps.

Wi-Fi Connection Issues

1. **Check Wi-Fi settings**: Go to **Settings** > **Wi-Fi** and make sure Wi-Fi is turned on. Ensure you're

connected to the correct network and that the network is working fine.

2. **Restart your router**: If your phone cannot connect to Wi-Fi, try restarting your Wi-Fi router. Sometimes the issue is with the router and not the phone.

3. **Forget and Reconnect to Wi-Fi**: Go to **Settings** > **Wi-Fi**, tap on the connected network, and choose **Forget**. Then, reconnect by selecting the network and entering the password.

4. **Check Wi-Fi signal strength**: Ensure you are within range of the Wi-Fi router and there are no obstacles (walls, electronics) blocking the signal.

5. **Update your device**: Sometimes, Wi-Fi issues can be resolved by a software update. Go to **Settings** > **System** > **Software updates** to check for any available updates.

Mobile Network Problems

1. **Toggle Airplane Mode**: Swipe down to access Quick Settings and turn on **Airplane Mode**. Wait for about 10 seconds, and then turn it off. This can often resolve network-related issues.

2. **Check Mobile Data Settings**: Go to **Settings** > **Network & Internet** > **Mobile network** and ensure **Mobile data** is enabled.

3. **Manually select network**: If your phone is not automatically connecting to your carrier's network, go to **Settings** > **Network & Internet** > **Mobile network** > **Advanced** > **Network operators**, and select your carrier manually.

Reset Network Settings

If all else fails, you can reset the network settings, which can resolve many connectivity issues:

1. Go to **Settings** > **System** > **Reset** > **Reset Wi-Fi, mobile & Bluetooth**.
2. Confirm the action and follow the on-screen instructions.

Tip: Resetting network settings will erase saved Wi-Fi networks, Bluetooth devices, and other network settings, so you'll need to reconnect to them afterward.

App Crashes and Freezing

If an app crashes or freezes on your Moto G Stylus 5G, follow these troubleshooting steps to resolve the issue.

Force Close the App

If an app freezes or becomes unresponsive:

1. Go to **Settings** > **Apps** > **See all apps**.
2. Find and tap on the app that's causing issues.
3. Tap **Force stop** to close the app. This will stop the app from running, and you can try reopening it.

Clear App Cache and Data

Sometimes, clearing an app's cache and data can resolve issues with crashing or freezing.

1. Go to **Settings** > **Apps** > **See all apps**.
2. Tap on the app that is malfunctioning.
3. Tap **Storage** and then select **Clear Cache** to remove temporary data. If the problem persists, try **Clear Data**, but note that this will reset the app to its default state and may remove any stored data.

Update the App

Outdated apps can sometimes cause crashes or freezing. Ensure the app is updated to the latest version:

1. Open the **Google Play Store**.
2. Tap the **three-line menu** icon and go to **My apps & games**.
3. Look for any apps with an **Update** button next to them and tap **Update**.

Uninstall and Reinstall the App

If clearing the cache and updating the app doesn't work:

1. Go to **Settings** > **Apps** > **See all apps**.
2. Tap on the app and select **Uninstall**.
3. Go to the **Google Play Store**, search for the app, and reinstall it.

Restart the Device

Sometimes a simple restart can resolve app issues:

1. Hold the **Power button** and tap **Restart**.
2. Once the device restarts, try opening the app again to see if it's working properly.

Chapter 17

Software Updates and Backups

Regularly updating your software and backing up your data are crucial for keeping your Moto G Stylus 5G running smoothly and securely. In this chapter, we'll guide you through checking for system updates, backing up your data, and performing a factory reset if needed.

Checking for System Updates

Keeping your phone's software up to date ensures that you benefit from the latest features, security patches, and bug fixes. Here's how to check for and install system updates on your Moto G Stylus 5G:

How to Check for Updates

1. Go to **Settings** > **System** > **Software updates**.
2. Your phone will automatically check for available updates. If an update is available, you will see a prompt to **Download and Install**.
3. Tap **Download** to start the process. The update may take some time, depending on your internet speed.
4. Once the download is complete, tap **Install**. The phone will restart and install the update.

Your Moto G Stylus 5G will notify you when a new update is available. If you prefer, you can also enable automatic updates by toggling on **Download updates automatically** in the update settings.

 Tip: It's best to connect to a Wi-Fi network before downloading a large system update to avoid using up your mobile data.

Backing Up Your Data

Backing up your data is important to ensure that your photos, contacts, apps, and other important files are safe. Here's how to back up your data on your Moto G Stylus 5G.

Using Google Backup

Google provides an easy way to back up your data to the cloud, including app data, contacts, calendar events, and more.

1. Go to **Settings** > **System** > **Backup**.
2. Toggle on **Back up to Google Drive**. This will enable automatic backup of:

- App data
- Call history
- Contacts
- Device settings
- Photos and videos (if using Google Photos)

Tip: For photos and videos, use the Google Photos app, which automatically backs up media when connected to Wi-Fi.

3. To perform an immediate backup, tap **Back Up Now**. It may take a few minutes depending on how much data you have.

Backing Up Photos and Videos

To ensure that your photos and videos are safely backed up:

1. Open the **Google Photos** app.
2. Tap on your profile icon in the top-right corner and select **Photo settings** > **Back up & sync**.
3. Turn on **Back up & sync**. This will automatically upload all your photos and videos to your Google account.

Backing Up Files Manually

If you prefer, you can back up files like documents, music, and other content manually to your Google Drive or an external SD card.

1. Open the **Files** app.
2. Select the files you want to back up and tap **Move** or **Copy**.
3. Choose **Google Drive** or an **SD card** as the destination and complete the transfer.

Factory Resetting the Phone

If you encounter persistent issues with your phone, or if you're preparing to sell or give away your device, a factory reset can restore your phone to its original settings by erasing all data.

Performing a Factory Reset

1. Go to **Settings** > **System** > **Reset** > **Erase all data (factory reset)**.
2. You'll be prompted to confirm the action. Tap **Erase Everything** to proceed.
3. The phone will reboot and begin the reset process. This may take several minutes.
4. After the reset, your phone will restart as if it were brand new, and you'll need to go through the initial setup process again.

Important Notes Before a Factory Reset

- **Backup your data**: A factory reset will erase everything from your device, including apps, contacts, and personal files. Make sure you have backed up important data to Google Drive or an external storage device.
- **Remove your Google account**: If you plan to sell or give away your phone, it's essential to remove your Google account to avoid issues with Factory Reset Protection (FRP). To do this, go to **Settings** > **Accounts** > **Google** > select your account > **Remove account**.

Chapter 18

Using the Moto App Features

The Moto G Stylus 5G offers a variety of unique features through the **Moto app**, designed to enhance your experience with gestures, displays, and customization options. In this chapter, we will cover Moto gestures and actions, Moto Display, Peek Display, and how to customize your phone with Moto Experiences.

Moto Gestures and Actions

Moto Gestures allow you to perform common tasks quickly by using simple, intuitive gestures on your phone. These can save you time and make your experience more fluid.

Common Moto Gestures

1. **Quick Capture**: To open the camera, quickly twist your wrist twice. This gesture works even when the phone is locked, so you can start taking pictures or videos instantly.
2. **Chop Chop for Flashlight**: To turn on the flashlight, quickly make a chopping motion with your hand. This will activate the flashlight even when the screen is off or the device is locked.

3. **Lift to Unlock**: Simply lift your phone to see notifications and unlock it. The display will automatically show you the lock screen or any important updates when you pick up the device.
4. **Double Tap to Sleep**: Tap the screen twice to put your phone to sleep without pressing the power button. This can be useful if you prefer not to use the physical buttons.

How to Enable or Customize Gestures

1. Open the **Moto app**.
2. Tap **Moto Actions**.
3. Toggle the gestures you want to use on or off, and follow the on-screen instructions to customize each gesture as desired.

Tip: Moto Gestures are customizable, so you can turn off the ones you don't use or adjust their settings to match your preferences.

Moto Display and Peek Display

Moto Display allows you to view important notifications, messages, and alerts without unlocking your phone. Peek Display is an extension of this feature that lets you see recent notifications by simply lifting your phone.

Moto Display

Moto Display allows your phone to show notifications and information on the lock screen in a way that saves battery life and prevents you from unlocking your device every time you get an alert.

- **Interactive Lock Screen**: When you receive notifications, your lock screen will show the app icon and a preview of the message.
- **Night Display**: Moto Display reduces the blue light emitted by the phone during nighttime, which helps reduce eye strain. You can enable this feature to automatically adjust the color temperature of your display at night.

Peek Display

Peek Display allows you to check recent notifications and messages without unlocking the phone. The phone briefly lights up when you pick it up, showing you recent alerts.

How to Enable Moto Display and Peek Display

1. Open the **Moto app**.
2. Tap **Moto Display**.
3. Toggle the **Peek Display** feature on to enable it.
4. Customize **Night Display** to activate at your preferred time (e.g., from 10:00 PM to 6:00 AM) to help reduce blue light exposure at night.

Tip: Peek Display is especially useful when you're trying to check notifications quickly without fully waking up your phone. It helps you keep track of your notifications without much effort.

Customizing with Moto Experiences

Moto Experiences give you the ability to customize and personalize your Moto G Stylus 5G, adding features and settings that make your phone feel truly yours.

Moto Actions (Previously Covered)

As part of Moto Experiences, **Moto Actions** allows you to control your device using gestures, making navigation easier and faster.

Moto Display (Previously Covered)

As discussed, **Moto Display** enhances your lock screen by providing notifications and information at a glance.

One Button Navigation

Moto G Stylus 5G also allows you to use **One Button Navigation**, which lets you navigate your phone using a single button instead of the traditional navigation buttons.

- **How it works**: Swipe up to go home, swipe and hold for recent apps, or swipe right/left to go back.
- You can enable **One Button Navigation** by going to **Settings** > **Display** > **Navigation** and selecting **One Button Navigation**.

Customization with Moto Themes

Moto G Stylus 5G includes several themes to customize the look of your device:

1. Open the **Moto app** and tap on **Moto Themes**.
2. Select a theme that changes your phone's appearance, such as different color schemes for your icons and system interface.

Display Customization

Moto Display's settings allow you to adjust brightness, add or remove widgets from the lock screen, and customize which types of notifications will appear.

Moto Actions for Enhanced Navigation

For users who prefer to reduce screen clutter, Moto Actions allows you to enable features like **One-Handed Mode**, making it easier to navigate the screen with one hand, or **Quick Launch** to open your favorite apps quickly by drawing a letter on the screen.

Chapter 19

Entertainment and Media

Your Moto G Stylus 5G is an excellent device for enjoying entertainment and media on the go. Whether you're listening to music, watching videos, streaming your favorite shows, or using FM radio, this chapter will guide you through the best features for media consumption on your phone.

Listening to Music and Podcasts

The Moto G Stylus 5G offers a variety of ways to enjoy music and podcasts. Whether you prefer streaming from online services, playing music stored on your phone, or using an FM radio, you have plenty of options.

Using Streaming Services (Spotify, YouTube Music, etc.)

1. **Spotify**: Download the **Spotify** app from the **Google Play Store** and log in or create an account. Once logged in, you can browse for playlists, albums, and songs, or use the **Spotify Free** service with ads or upgrade to **Spotify Premium** for an ad-free experience.
2. **YouTube Music**: Download the **YouTube Music** app to listen to millions of songs, albums, and playlists. Like Spotify, it offers both free and premium versions.

3. **Apple Music**: If you're an Apple Music subscriber, you can also download and use the **Apple Music** app for streaming music.

To listen to music on these apps, simply open the app, select your preferred song or playlist, and press play.

Listening to Podcasts

1. **Google Podcasts**: This free app is pre-installed on most Android devices, including the Moto G Stylus 5G. Simply open **Google Podcasts** and search for your favorite podcasts or browse categories.
2. **Spotify and Other Podcast Apps**: Apps like Spotify, Stitcher, or Pocket Casts are great options for listening to podcasts. Simply download the app, browse or search for podcasts, and listen to them at your convenience.

Playing Music Stored on Your Phone

If you have music files saved directly on your phone, you can play them using the **Google Play Music** app or any other third-party music player, such as **VLC** or **AIMP**.

1. Open the **Google Play Music** or your chosen music player app.
2. Browse or search for the song, album, or playlist you want to play.
3. Tap to play and adjust the volume using the phone's physical volume buttons.

Connecting Bluetooth Speakers or Headphones

To enjoy your music with better sound quality, you can connect your phone to Bluetooth speakers or headphones:

1. Go to **Settings** > **Bluetooth**.
2. Turn on Bluetooth and make sure your speakers or headphones are in pairing mode.
3. Tap on the name of your device to pair it with the phone.
4. Once connected, you can enjoy your music wirelessly!

Watching Videos and Streaming

The Moto G Stylus 5G features a large, vibrant display perfect for watching videos and streaming your favorite shows. Whether you're using YouTube, Netflix, or other streaming apps, your phone provides an excellent viewing experience.

Streaming with YouTube

1. Open the **YouTube** app on your phone.
2. Log in to your Google account (if necessary) and browse for videos or channels you like.
3. Tap on a video to start watching. You can change the video quality by tapping on the three dots in the top-right corner of the video player and selecting **Quality**.
4. You can also subscribe to channels, create playlists, and save videos to watch later.

Streaming Services (Netflix, Hulu, Disney+, etc.)

To watch movies and TV shows, you can use popular streaming apps like **Netflix**, **Hulu**, **Disney+**, or **Amazon Prime Video**. Download the apps from the **Google Play Store** and sign in with your account.

1. Open the app and browse through content categories.
2. Tap on a movie or show to start watching.
3. Use the on-screen controls to pause, play, adjust the volume, or switch the video quality.

Casting Videos to a Bigger Screen (Chromecast)

If you have a **Chromecast** or a TV with **Chromecast built-in**, you can cast videos from your Moto G Stylus 5G to a larger screen. Here's how:

1. Make sure both your phone and TV are connected to the same Wi-Fi network.
2. Open a streaming app like YouTube or Netflix.
3. Tap the **Cast icon** (usually a small TV screen with waves) and select your Chromecast-enabled device.
4. The video will start playing on your TV, and you can control playback directly from your phone.

Using the Moto G Stylus 5G Display

The phone's large screen makes it ideal for streaming, so be sure to adjust the screen settings for the best viewing experience. To enhance your display:

1. Go to **Settings** > **Display** > **Display size** to make the text and icons larger for easier viewing.
2. Enable **Night Display** if you're watching at night, which reduces blue light to prevent eye strain.

Using FM Radio and YouTube

The Moto G Stylus 5G comes with a built-in FM radio feature, allowing you to listen to local radio stations without using mobile data or Wi-Fi. You can also enjoy YouTube and other video content through the app.

Listening to FM Radio

1. Open the **FM Radio** app on your phone (you may need to install a third-party FM radio app from the **Google Play Store** if it's not pre-installed).
2. Connect a pair of wired headphones (they act as the antenna for the FM radio).
3. Open the app, and you should be able to start tuning into your favorite local radio stations.
4. Use the dialer to search for stations and save your favorites for easy access.

 Tip: Make sure you're in an area with a strong signal for the best FM radio reception.

YouTube for Music Videos, Shows, and More

In addition to regular video content, **YouTube** is a great source for music videos, vlogs, and other forms of entertainment. Open the app and browse for your favorite content, whether it's a trending video, a live stream, or something you've saved to your playlists.

Chapter 20

Staying Safe Online

In today's digital age, it's essential to stay vigilant when browsing the internet and using your Moto G Stylus 5G. This chapter will guide you through recognizing scams and spam, practicing safe browsing habits, and using parental controls to protect younger users.

Recognizing Scams and Spam

Scams and spam are common online threats that can compromise your privacy, security, and finances. Being able to recognize them can help you avoid falling victim to fraud.

Recognizing Scam Emails and Messages

1. **Suspicious Email Addresses**: Phishing emails often come from addresses that look similar to legitimate ones but have slight variations. Always check the sender's email carefully.
2. **Urgent or Threatening Language**: Scammers often use phrases like "urgent," "your account is compromised," or "immediate action required." Be cautious of messages that pressure you to act quickly.
3. **Suspicious Links and Attachments**: Never click on links or open attachments from unknown sources. Hover over a link to see if the URL looks legitimate.

Be wary of any email asking you to click a link or provide sensitive information.

4. **Too Good to Be True Offers**: If you receive an offer that sounds too good to be true, it probably is. Be cautious of messages claiming you've won a prize or offer that requires personal information or payment.

5. **Unsolicited Requests for Personal Information**: Legitimate companies typically don't ask for sensitive personal information (like passwords or credit card details) via email or text.

Recognizing Spam Messages

1. **Generic Greetings**: Spam messages may use vague greetings like "Dear Customer" instead of addressing you by name.

2. **Excessive Ads**: If you receive unsolicited messages promoting products, it's likely spam.

3. **Too Many Unsubscribed Messages**: If you're receiving more promotional emails than usual, consider unsubscribing from irrelevant mailing lists.

What to Do If You Receive a Scam or Spam Message

1. **Do Not Respond**: Avoid replying to any scam or spam message.

2. **Report the Message**: Many email services and messaging apps allow you to report suspicious messages. Use these features to alert the service providers.

3. **Delete the Message**: If you're unsure whether a message is legitimate, it's best to delete it rather than open any links or attachments.

Safe Browsing Tips

Practicing safe browsing habits is key to protecting your privacy and security while online. Here are some important tips to keep in mind.

Using a Secure Network

- Always connect to a secure Wi-Fi network that requires a password. Public Wi-Fi networks are often not encrypted, making it easier for malicious actors to intercept your data.
- If you're unsure about a network's security, use mobile data to browse instead.

Avoiding Unsecure Websites

- Look for a **padlock icon** in the URL bar before entering personal information on a website. This indicates that the site uses **HTTPS** encryption to protect your data.
- Avoid entering sensitive information on websites that don't show a padlock icon, as they may not be secure.

Using Private Browsing (Incognito Mode)

- Use **Incognito Mode** or **Private Browsing** when accessing websites you don't want to be saved in your browser history. This feature is especially useful when researching sensitive topics or shopping online.

- To enable **Incognito Mode** in Google Chrome, tap the three dots in the top-right corner of the browser and select **New Incognito Tab**.

Clearing Your Browsing History

- Regularly clear your browser history, cookies, and cached data to prevent your browsing habits from being tracked.
- To clear browsing data in Google Chrome:
    1. Open Chrome and tap the three dots in the top-right corner.
    2. Tap **History**, then **Clear browsing data**.
    3. Select the types of data you want to delete, such as history, cookies, and cache.

Using a VPN (Virtual Private Network)

- A VPN encrypts your internet connection and hides your IP address, making it harder for third parties to track your online activities. Consider using a VPN when browsing public Wi-Fi networks or when privacy is a concern.

Using Parental Controls

If you have children or younger family members using your Moto G Stylus 5G, setting up parental controls is essential to ensure they have a safe and age-appropriate experience online.

Google Family Link allows you to manage and monitor your child's device usage, including screen time, app usage, and online activity.

1. **Set Up Google Family Link**:

   - Download the **Google Family Link** app from the **Google Play Store**.
   - Follow the on-screen instructions to create a family group and link your child's device.

2. **Managing Apps and Screen Time**:

   - Once Family Link is set up, you can approve or block apps that your child tries to download.
   - You can also set time limits for app usage and lock the device remotely when it's time to take a break.

Using Device-Specific Parental Controls

1. **Google Play Store Restrictions**:

   - Open the **Google Play Store** app.
   - Tap the **profile icon** in the top-right corner and select **Settings > Parental controls**.
   - Toggle on **Parental controls** and set restrictions for apps, games, and media based on age ratings.

2. **Restricted Content in YouTube**:

   - Open the **YouTube** app and go to **Settings > General**.

113

- Enable **Restricted Mode** to filter out potentially mature content.

Blocking Websites or Apps

1. **Blocking Websites**: You can block certain websites through the Family Link app or by using third-party parental control apps like **Qustodio** or **Norton Family**.
2. **App Restrictions**: You can restrict access to specific apps by either using Family Link or built-in restrictions in the **Settings** menu.

Chapter 21

Helpful Tips and Tricks

Your Moto G Stylus 5G is packed with advanced features designed to make your experience smoother and more enjoyable. In this chapter, we'll cover some helpful tips and tricks to enhance your productivity, streamline tasks, and uncover hidden features that will make using your phone even more fun.

Screenshot and Screen Recording

Capturing your screen can be useful for sharing important information, saving content, or troubleshooting issues. The Moto G Stylus 5G makes it easy to take screenshots and record your screen.

Taking a Screenshot

1. **Method 1**: Press the **Power** button and the **Volume Down** button at the same time, hold for a moment, and your phone will capture the current screen.
2. **Method 2**: Use **Three-Finger Swipe** (available on certain Moto phones):

- Go to **Settings > Gestures > Three-finger screenshot**.
- Enable the feature and swipe down with three fingers to capture a screenshot.

- After taking a screenshot, you'll see a preview of the image at the bottom of the screen. You can edit or share it directly from there.

Screen Recording

1. **Method 1**: Swipe down to open the **Quick Settings** menu.
2. Tap the **Screen Record** icon (it may be hidden behind the edit button; swipe down again to reveal all icons).
3. Select whether to record audio, and then press **Start** to begin recording your screen.
4. To stop recording, swipe down again and tap the **Stop** button. The video will be saved to your **Gallery**.

Tip: You can use screen recording for tutorials, capturing gameplay, or documenting a process to share with others.

Split Screen and Multitasking

The Moto G Stylus 5G supports **split-screen mode**, which lets you use two apps side-by-side, making multitasking much easier.

Using Split Screen Mode

1. Open the first app you want to use.
2. Tap the **Recent Apps** button (the square icon).
3. Find the app you want to use in split-screen and tap on the **app icon** at the top of the preview.
4. Select **Split screen** from the menu.

5. Choose the second app from your recent apps or open an app from the **App Drawer** to use it in the second window.
6. You can adjust the size of the apps by dragging the divider up or down.

Switching Apps in Split Screen

- To switch one of the apps, tap the **Recent Apps** button again, choose a new app, and drag it to the other side of the screen.
- To exit split-screen mode, drag the divider all the way to the top or bottom.

Tip: Split screen is great for multitasking, such as checking your email while watching a video or browsing the web while messaging a friend.

Hidden Features You Should Know

Your Moto G Stylus 5G has some lesser-known features that can enhance your experience. These hidden gems can improve efficiency, privacy, and fun.

One-Handed Mode

If you prefer to use your phone with one hand, Moto G Stylus 5G has a **one-handed mode** that shrinks the screen size for easier navigation.

1. Go to **Settings** > **Display** > **One-Handed Mode**.
2. Toggle the feature on and adjust the size of the screen for more comfortable one-handed use.

Moto Actions (Quick Launch, Chop Chop)

We mentioned some Moto gestures earlier, but here's a quick reminder of a few more that can boost your productivity:

- **Quick Launch**: Open the camera by twisting your wrist twice (even when the phone is locked).
- **Chop Chop for Flashlight**: Activate the flashlight by making a chopping motion with your hand.
- **Flip to Mute**: Flip the phone face down to mute incoming calls or notifications.

Double Tap to Wake Up

Enable **Double Tap to Wake** so you don't have to press the power button to check the time, notifications, or quickly access your home screen.

1. Go to **Settings** > **Display** > **Double Tap to Wake**.
2. Toggle the option on.

Night Light and Blue Light Filter

At night, use the **Night Light** feature to reduce blue light exposure, which can help you sleep better.

1. Go to **Settings** > **Display** > **Night Light**.
2. Toggle the feature on and adjust the schedule (e.g., activate from 10 PM to 6 AM).

Game Mode for Better Gaming

Your Moto G Stylus 5G includes a **Gaming Mode** to reduce interruptions and improve performance while playing games:

1. Open **Settings** > **Gaming**.
2. Enable **Do Not Disturb** to block notifications during gameplay.
3. You can also adjust the performance settings to optimize gameplay, depending on the game you're playing.

Charging the Phone Faster (Battery Saver)

Use **Battery Saver** mode to extend battery life during a long day of use:

1. Go to **Settings** > **Battery** > **Battery Saver**.
2. Toggle the feature on to reduce battery consumption by limiting background processes and notifications.
3. Enable **Adaptive Battery** to allow the phone to learn your usage patterns and save battery accordingly.

Chapter 22

Appendix and FAQs

In this final chapter, we'll cover some helpful reference material, including a glossary of common terms, answers to frequently asked questions, and where to find customer support and additional resources. This section is designed to provide quick access to helpful information whenever you need it.

Glossary of Common Terms

Understanding some common technical terms can make using your Moto G Stylus 5G much easier. Here's a quick reference guide to help you familiarize yourself with key terminology.

- **Android OS**: The operating system that runs on your Moto G Stylus 5G, developed by Google.
- **SIM Card**: A small card that allows your phone to connect to a cellular network for calls and data.
- **SD Card**: A removable storage device used to expand the memory of your phone.
- **Wi-Fi**: A wireless network technology that allows your phone to connect to the internet without using mobile data.
- **Bluetooth**: A wireless technology that allows you to connect to other devices like headphones, speakers, and smartwatches.

- **Screen Resolution**: The clarity of the display, typically measured in pixels (e.g., Full HD).
- **GPS (Global Positioning System)**: A system that allows your phone to determine your location.
- **App Drawer**: A menu that shows all the apps installed on your device.
- **Battery Saver**: A feature that reduces battery usage by limiting background activities.
- **Firmware**: The software that is permanently programmed into your phone's hardware.
- **Rooting**: The process of unlocking your phone to gain full access to its operating system.

Frequently Asked Questions (FAQs)

Here are some common questions users have about the Moto G Stylus 5G. If you're experiencing a problem or need further clarification, check here for solutions.

Q1: How do I extend the battery life of my Moto G Stylus 5G?

To improve battery life, enable **Battery Saver**, reduce screen brightness, turn off unused features like Bluetooth and Wi-Fi when not in use, and avoid running multiple apps in the background.

Q2: How do I take a screenshot?

Press the **Power** button and **Volume Down** button simultaneously to capture a screenshot. Alternatively, enable the **Three-Finger Screenshot** gesture in **Settings** for an easier capture.

Q3: How do I enable split-screen multitasking?

To use split-screen mode, open the first app, then tap the **Recent Apps** button. Tap the app icon at the top of the preview and select **Split screen**. Choose a second app from your recent apps or app drawer to use side-by-side.

Q4: What is Moto Display, and how do I use it?

Moto Display allows you to view notifications without unlocking your phone. It lights up when you receive a new notification or when you pick up your device. You can enable it by going to **Settings** > **Moto** > **Moto Display**.

Q5: How do I set up my Google account?

To set up your Google account, go to **Settings** > **Accounts** > **Add account** > **Google**. Follow the prompts to either sign in with an existing Google account or create a new one.

Q6: How do I factory reset my phone?

To perform a factory reset, go to **Settings** > **System** > **Reset** > **Factory data reset**. This will erase all data from your device, so make sure to back up your important files beforehand.

Q7: Can I use the Moto G Stylus 5G for gaming?

Yes, the Moto G Stylus 5G is capable of gaming. To optimize performance, enable **Game Mode** in **Settings** > **Gaming** and adjust the settings for a smoother experience.

Customer Support and Resources

If you need further assistance, there are various resources available to you for troubleshooting, repairs, or questions about your Moto G Stylus 5G.

Official Motorola Support

- **Website**: Motorola Support
- **Live Chat**: Available on the Motorola support website for real-time assistance.
- **Phone Support**: Contact Motorola's customer service at 1-800-734-5870 (available in the U.S.).
- **Email Support**: Email support is available through the **Contact Us** page on the Motorola website.

Online Communities and Forums

- **Motorola Community**: Visit the Motorola Community Forums to ask questions, share tips, and connect with other Moto users.
- **Reddit**: There are various subreddits like r/Motorola where you can get advice and support from other Moto users.

Motorola Authorized Service Centers

If your phone requires repair or replacement, visit an authorized Motorola service center. You can find a list of authorized service centers on the official Motorola website.

Your Moto G Stylus 5G comes with a standard manufacturer's warranty, which covers defects in materials and workmanship. For detailed warranty coverage and how to file a claim, visit the **Warranty Information** section of Motorola's website.

Software Updates

To ensure your device is always up to date, go to **Settings > System > Updates** to check for software updates. Installing the latest updates will improve performance and security.

www.ingramcontent.com/pod-product-compliance
Lightning Source LLC
Chambersburg PA
CBHW052147070326
40689CB00050B/2405